*Whilst Walking Away*

# *Whilst Walking Away*

## poetry and prose

## Rowan J. Paige

Publisher Jessica Walker

# *Contents*

For Sarah--my partner, my muse, and my biggest supporter. You are my home, no matter where life takes us.

To Kristen for always believing in me.

To Harry, the deer who let me sit with him in silence when I really needed a friend.

# *Author's Notes*

I wrote *Whilst Gazing* three years ago at the start of the pandemic when the small business I worked for closed down along with the rest of the world. I found myself gazing through windows, daydreaming, and finding an escape from... everything, including all of the nothingness. Suddenly, colors were feelings. Trees were friends. The weather was entertainment. Then, one day, I was busy again-- walking past trees as if they were only trees and nothing more. I wasn't gazing. I glanced from time to time but wasn't seeing the world the same way.

When my life became about work, money, and pushing sales, I stopped writing for myself. Most of my creativity was used for branding. I needed a new environment and disruption to my routine. I needed to walk away from the things causing my mental health and quality of life to suffer. So, I did. I moved three thousand miles away from the Gulf Coast to the Pacific North West. Since my wife, pets, and I crossed the country and started a brand-new life, I have seen so many breathtaking things I never imagined existed in my wildest dreams: Enormous trees and gigantic waves, fog that dances in the morning light. The smallest birds and creatures quickly became companions. The mesmerizing ocean views became a symbol of safety.

I wanted to write about all of it.

I wanted to capture the magic because I was afraid I could lose it.

I was lost, but somehow I was finding more than I ever knew was missing. I was home in a place unknown to me.

This book is about that journey. The joy. The fear. The homesickness. Every season. Every new revelation and getting lost along the way.

# Author's Notes

# ONE

# *Coffee Break Contemplations*

**March 25, 2021**

I will write a whole book
before I step another foot
back into this place.

I was at a time in my life when I felt incredibly stuck in a position I was not capable to fill. I was in over my head, drowning in responsibilities far too heavy for me. I remember a day I considered walking away from everything—life itself—because I would rather disappear from the picture than quit my job. I needed financial stability but it was causing my mental stability to crumble. I was experiencing physical pain and discomfort constantly, I was losing sleep. I was having dark thoughts, really dark thoughts. I had a total nervous breakdown one morning before work and thankfully my partner calmed me down and gave me permission and encouragement to finally walk away from that job. It wasn't worth it. Management was aware I was struggling and they simply did not care enough to offer me any help. They only gave me more responsibility with little to no assistance and chose to ignore all the signs right in front of them that I was not okay. No one deserves that. No one deserves to be ignored and used and taken advantage of. Work should not feel like a place of fear. I realized I deserve encouragement, support, and acknowledgment. I deserved to have a better quality of life. Walking away from that place gave me the freedom to create a better life for myself and I now see that sometimes it is okay to quit. To give up. To walk away. That day, I started writing this book! I never walked back into that building again.

## SURE THING

dancing around in circles
i can feel myself slip away
beside myself
everything feels unstable in times like these
but you hold me tight and tell me
we're a sure thing
our home and the family we made
when the world is falling apart
we're a sure thing

# MAYBE IN THE NEXT LIFE

I can't be the only one
Surely I'm not the first
To want to be a tree
Basking in the morning light
Dancing in the dawn
To the soft, sweet song of the chickadee
(They speed along from limb to limb so freely)
A sort of freedom I will never know but always seek
November forenoon gleams with vermilion leaves
Enormous pines stand steady in the background
The half-moon stares back at me, stoic as ever
I take a sip of coffee and sigh
Maybe in the next life.

untitled

I confess my pain with a twitching mouth
and you have the audacity
to stack more stress on my plate
soaked in fatty false-flattery
and salted with my sweat for flavor
we both know I'm disposable
a number to carry your weight
and so you dance on my last nerve
as if I grow them in my back garden

## SOMEWHERE ELSE

I'm so much more like me
Undeniably free
When I'm high in the trees
Mountains wait for me
The sea waves in a plea
There's something I need to see
Somewhere else I need to be

*I quit...*

I quit bending for your pleasure
I quit breaking for your amusement
I quit putting myself on the back burner
I quit putting my dreams on hold
I quit biting my tongue just to feed it

Today I don't just quit...
I start putting myself first for the very first time
If I go hungry, it won't be for long
because I'd be full everywhere that you drained me

## WINTER BLUES

wine lingers
shaking fingers
attempt to tie
a knot
or knit a sweater
to ride the weather
until the fire dies, hot
dry eyes
look forward still
the moon is my guide
every cycle brings me closer
to Spring's wet inside

## SWADDLE

Wrap my mind in white
linen drapery
Swaddle my thoughts
And rock them to sleep

NOTICE

Your two weeks notice was two weeks ago
when I cried in the lobby
and in front of a window
because I was so tired I didn't care if anyone was to see
(I hoped someone might)
That's all the notice you needed...
but you didn't notice me at all

Leslie Gore said it best
When she shouted that line
And pounded her chest
**You don't own me**

It's easy to forget that you are free
sometimes
when there's a fee to live
— a fee to die
— a fee to survive

# MOURNING ROUTINE

I brush my teeth between breakdowns
Combing my hair with shaky fingers
Fingers that are tired
But tired isn't sick enough
Afraid isn't sick enough
So I gargle and spit and take another pill
This is my mourning routine.

Shutdown breakdown – April 6, 2020

yesterday i finally broke
i cried
over a cup of tea
in the shower
during dinner
and before bed
but it was a breakthrough nonetheless

## Coffee Break Contemplating

The trees look deliciously green
as I envy the birds on my lunch break
Look how free they are
Free to fly without the weight
of bills to pay or a man to answer to
I sip on stale coffee and stir the cream
like I stir the idea of leaving
around and around until the colour turns tan
and the coffee is more palatable
And I ponder the thought
That this clock-out could be the last
I place my mind on the left plate
and money on the right
The scale tells no lies...
Punching my card doesn't keep me alive
any more than a bird needs permission to fly

I wish I were a Rainbow

They don't believe in me...
I know.
I wish I were like a rainbow.
A rare sign of hope.
Something treasured.
Something wished upon.

Would it be so bad to disappear into the wild unknown
Start over fresh and find a place to call home?

## Another Depressive Wave

My mind is too intertwined
I'm running out of time
In my dreams, I won't survive
I need to get out of this place
I don't recognize my own face
I'm far from happy here
I'm tired and exhausted from fear
Is this another depressive wave?
Or a sign to finally escape?

# Time to Fly

Same old
Same old
Craving something new to hold
This chapter is drug out
Rung dry
Wake me when its time to fly

Wedding Day

The morning of my wedding
was one of the best few hours of my life
I woke in Forks, Washington
It was the end of May
I sat outside on the back deck
Where our reception was taking place that night
The sun was as soft as silk
The mist was lightly grazing the tips of the treeline

I wrote my vows, sipping coffee and mimosa
I saw a rabbit walking by
A bald eagle scanning the sky
I felt at home
I didn't want to leave that space
It was magic
I knew it to be true

I was happy, really happy
I didn't want to ever forget how that felt
Now I never will

I imagined my new life out there
Waking up to that view every day
I was finally going to be in a place that suits my soul
With the person who loves it most

## Mystery Carries Them By

Somehow the pigeons seem like they know a secret
A happy mystery carries them by

# TWO

## *Renewal*

I want to be where the mountains are
Where the air is crisp and the waters are calm
Take me where the trees stand like soldiers
And the stars shine like gems across the velvet sky
Home is where the heart is they say
And my heart is with the Wild

## My Favorite Color

I thought I knew green
until I saw the way her eyes looked
against the rich mossy backdrop
of the Pacific Northwest
I knew then it was my favorite color.

# Breathing

I took a breath and it was easy
The air was smooth and it tasted sweet
I took a breath
I inhaled deeply
and let it go for the wind to sweep

Today I saw a deer. Not just any deer but a huge buck that was grazing just outside my kitchen window. I always thought that was a nice place for a deer and there he was. Having a late breakfast as I was making my coffee.

## DAZED in the SUMMER HIVE

Picture us back when we were nimble and spry...
a honeysuckle-coated backdrop
under the hazy twilight
Remember how crickets cried out...
in a constant chorus of love-making and strife
We could run like the wind
until we laughed 'til we cried
I can still taste the bitter august blues
and how they stood the test of time,
time and time again we said our goodbyes...
Pen to paper until the bloody ink ran dry
but I never forgot the way you smiled with your eyes,
so bottomless and bright but filled with brine
Picture us dazed in the summer hive
we felt loved and infinite and we felt alive

## SEPTEMBER CAME LIKE A DREAM

As the wind swept across the cold grey sky,

the clouds curled in on themselves with tails like wispy feathers.

September came like a dream on a restless night--

with a painfully slow cooling of Summer, then a sudden drop

into the orange moonlit nights of early autumn.

The sky is colored livid like the skin beneath my eyes, and my hair,

a shade of rich umber, curls in the mistful breeze...

Bewitchingly, the coast has been coated

with dense fog that dances elegantly in the morning sunrise,

and peace washes soon over me like a blanket in the night.

I woke in a meadow at the base of a great mountain
Ice covered the grass like glass
The lake was still and blue like the sky
The hills were a pink I've yet to see again
Sun easing her way to the top
I remember feeling like it was all for me
Just for a morning

## SHEILA BEAT ME AT SCRABBLE

Sheila beat me at Scrabble on a Tuesday night
That was the first time I felt alright,
comfortable in my own skin
No matter the words said
from my next of kin...
I remember so clearly how she lit incense to burn
Oh, how I yearned to be ignited by her...
It smelled of sage and apples as the fumes rose high
Peach bourbon was poured generously,
then topped with cubes of ice
My fingers were cold but happier still
because she had touched them
it gave me a chill
It was a boiling wet Tuesday in early July
Humidity clung to our skin like white on rice
and the sky was still streaked with firework smoke
I thought I could die when she laughed at my joke
The grass was green and damp
as it grazed my calves
and the fireflies provided the ambiance
as they danced and danced
Sheila had just chopped her auburn hair
and it took everything in me not to stare
*I like your new look,*
I said with a smile
*Thank you, my dear,*
Oh, I swear I could fly...
As the turntable spun Stevie Ray Vaughn

Sheila tapped her feet as she hummed along
I don't know that I had ever felt quite as free
to be loved
to be heard
and to really be seen
Sheila beat me at Scrabble on a Tuesday night
For the very first time, I felt alright

# SPRING LOOMS ON THE HORIZON

Moisture clings to my skin
latching onto every square-inch
until all of me is covered and drenched
in honeysuckle-sucking days of Lent
Spring looms on the horizon
Hot and sultry with suffocating breath
that smells of young violets
Humidity pulls at the ends of my curls
like a game of Tug of War
Dew-speckled grass grown above my kneecaps
tickles and teases and itches for play
as wisteria blooms and stretches across the archway
Rain raps on the roof and the sizzling pavement
turning to mist that creates fog-infested riverbanks
April has cast her wretched love spell once more
Consider yourself duly warned

## BLUE VEINS

deep blue feels like *home*
something i trust, something i know
ever since i was a child, i could see it
feel it in the comfort of rich indigo
that calms my senses, eases my nerves
i swaddle my mind with blue memories
and let my dreams take flight
my blue veins run vibrant
as the cool blood flows
i am one with the sky
and at peace with the ocean tide
Blue is peaceful and present
understanding and open to change
and sometimes if you close your eyes
Blue is a wise flame
i am *Blue*, daughter of the moonlit night
you can see it in my veins
you can see it in my eyes

November rolled in with yellow, crisp leaves clinging for dear life on the ends of the branches of golden-rod trees. The wind shot through the cracked window, flying into the gaps in my jacket. I tugged at my sleeves as my hair lifted into the air and my ears burned. The delightful sting of Autumn had arrived. A soft rain fell outside the window. The kind you don't really notice unless you look up.

The trees shimmy and shake their limbs,
doing the Mambo to the beat of the ocean's song
Bending their branches
and turning their leaves into maracas,
they dance and dance until the sultry sun
settles below the bay
and the moon calls the world to rest

*Summer in the Pacific North West*

# THE FIRST OF MAY (WAS A COIN TOSS)

The first of May was a coin-toss
You were on the fray, like dental floss
But I held you tight as you melted into liquid gold
The snow came down and we caught a cold
Hot toddies by the fire
We were shut in, close
nowhere else to go
Billie playing quiet on the radio
In our bunker, we were safe and warm
The first of May was a coin toss
that landed on love and white frost

## SNUFF

I worry about her when the sky is overcast and grey
Maybe she won't have enough light to see the way
I light another candle and tell her
She can snuff it when she's ready

As I take an honest look around me, opening my s[e]
to my new environment, I feel as though I am still dreaming.
I can see the ducks sunbathing, I can smell the sweet scent
of pine and freshly cut lawn, and I can taste this oddly
distinctive taste of crisp, fresh air. The sound of the birds
conversing all around me and the chitter-chatter of families
strolling together is something from a romantic comedy
when the protagonist is to be going for a run or a walk with
her puppy. I don't know. It feels too good... a good I've never
really felt or seen or touched. But, here I am and I can touch
the grass and the bark of the tall trees and I know that this
is real. I'm home.


The white and yellow weeds dust the sweetly scented, green
lawn. Everything is so lush, and green that I'm afraid I'm
looking through rose-tinted glasses- or worse, dreaming.
The cool air feels amazing, blowing gently through my hair.
It's nearly July, and in Alabama, this would feel like a cold
front... Hell surely freezing over. I packed a sweater in my
backpack for when the evening came and I'm thrilled that I
can still wear my favorite layered clothes in Summer here.

# JUNE IN THE COOS

Subtle notes of sweet pine float
In with the crisp breeze
And land gently on my nose
It's difficult to believe
This is meant to be Spring...
Chartreuse leaves bounce and bob above–
Draped against the buttery clouded sky.
I exhale as a crow calls from across
The prickled path of pines.

I wrote "June In The Coos" the first week we arrived in our new home. I was mesmerized by how soft and easy the air was to breathe. I was used to Spring being unbearable, but here I was relishing in it all. I fell in love with June. I never thought it was a possibility. Usually, this would be the start of my Seasonal Depression, but instead, I was so calm and at peace and comfortable. I knew then that we had come to the right place. We made a good choice. I was going to be happy here.

## I WISH IT WOULD RAIN...

I wish it would rain
He said as we sat hand in hand
On the park bench on a Tuesday
Overcast skies, deliciously grey
Not to ruin this date
Everything about this moment
Is so perfect
If only it would rain
And we could run to shelter
Fast and clumsily
We could laugh our way through the door
And up the wooden staircase
To your bedroom and warm sheets
Undressing
And pressing
Our warm lips together
*If only it would rain...*

# PROLIFIC

Brown dirt
damp and rich
Matches her downturned eyes
Plum purple kisses her lips
Like dark violets
bloom in late winter
Her hair grows like a vine
spun out and intertwined
In the Spring she sings like a Nightingale
She sways like the limbs of a tree
Green with envy,
Willows cry for her
She is more alive than water is prolific
She is freedom in human form
Conversing with the moon
like an old friend over tea
When she cries her eyes are clouds
Sobs fall from her mouth
like leaves dropping in Autumn
My love is a biophilic woman
Her body is a raging river
winding and temperamental
but a soothing comfort at night

## Blue Velvet Sweater

cappuccino steam rises as i sip
golden crema tastes like butter on my lips
fog flows and mist falls
as the brown leaves scatter across
the sky so grey
my sweater is blue velvet
soft and safe
matching my eyes and the sky
in October's harvest prime
on a Wednesday morning fresh and full
of restful intentions
calm coziness spreads
throughout my homestead
my kitten purrs quietly

Bird Watching:

as the wind blows
the trees sway
birds caw out in joy
flying fast and free
i think secretly
i wish i were a bird
i wish i were of the blue
of the wild
and the serene

February's Full Moon

The Snow Moon falls to sleep
To the steps the ice clings
In the morning we hike uphill
Soft powder beneath our heels
The trees have been generously sugared
Every inch dusted for her
Winter turns our fingers pink
Indoors we share a warm drink
February finds us well
Under her frosted lover spell

## SHUT-IN

The moonlight peeps in through the curtains
as the fire pops and cracks, filling the room with warmth
as the world begins to fall asleep
Another Sunday evening finds us at home
cuddling close together
Couch potatoes huddled and bundled tight
wrapped in a fuzzy blanket and covered in fur
You sip on red wine as a movie flickers on the screen
I belly laugh and the cat snores obnoxiously

Times like these feel as though
there is no one else on Earth
but us,
our family
safe and sound and completely content
Moments like this remind me that nothing else,
no one else, matters
but you and me and our snoring cat...
In quarantine

August, hello

Suddenly the cool wind against my skin feels different from any breeze I've ever felt before... I've never noticed how incredible branches this large look when they sway– so strongly they creak, and you're almost afraid one will snap and fall. It's mesmerizing. The leaves are a completely new shade of green. A color previously unknown to me in any way other than television and film. Deep. Rich. Strikingly green. So captivating and vibrant, I don't know where to direct my attention.

The sun settles on the back of my neck, and the coastal air twirls the hair against my face. My body is completely content with the weather. I've never known an August like this.

## ELLE EST CHALEUR

Elle est chaleur
She is warmth
Réconfort
Inviting like a candle in a window
on a crisp night in October
Cold nose
Frozen toes
but some warm drink will do just fine
to defrost my mind
and relax my thighs
She is as gentle as a breeze on a coastline
when she loves you at night
Eager to keep you safe and warm
and free from harm
She's a refuge
a strong, fierce knight
to be rescued by her is a delight
Peace of mind
She goes against the tide
for you to be by her side
Elle est chaleur
She is warmth

## MORNING

Morning glory, just outside my kitchen window, wave
hello
My coffee sits, ice melting,
as I forget once again what I entered this room for

## She Was The Summer They Write About In Books

I met her in a dusty record shop
It was a sultry day on the boardwalk
She asked me about the bus route,
then for hours on we still talked...
Her voice was pastel and her mouth was soft
Eyes speckled with green and yellow dots
I mustered all of my confidence
and invited her up to my cheap loft
Hair like honey and a heart of gold
I melted for her like butter on a stove
she made my Summer one I still hold
Close to my heart with endless love
She was the Summer they write about in books
She had a fire for soul and a garden for looks

Pretty Pacific Blue

Saturday beckons with orange sunlight
creeping into the stairwell
an open window welcomes fresh pine-scented wind
The clouds are transparent as the sky beams
in pretty pacific blue.

Poems about Mountains

Here i am
Again
Writing poems about mountains
That i envy
Because they are magical
And big and powerful
And worthy of seeking
Hiking towards
Fighting for

## FLOCK

My god how badly i want to be a part of a flock
A cluster sweeping the edges of the water

At Midnight in December

Little pinecones litter the ground
Not a sound is heard then
At midnight in December
Just the freezing of limbs so bare
And leaves rotting, molding into dirt
Somehow everything seems okay on the Winter nights
When the stars are at their brightest
And the trees are dying fast

Toasted Glaze

This morning i don't feel like i have much else to say
Instead, I'm just going to make some coffee and daydream
Sunlight caresses the nape of my neck
The Sunday is spruced with toasted glaze

*Sugary Crackling Candles*

I'll keep lighting my sugary crackling candles
while I stare out of windows
As long as it makes me feel a little more alive
than i do when i'm living
Living takes it out of me like hiking a treeless hill in July
Forest fire smoke makes my asthma flare up
like depression in January
So I light my fancy long matches
and draw the curtains back
And i breathe in and out
until Monday rises from the heap

*cornflower*

I thought I knew blue,
until I saw cornflowers
dancing at high noon.

Oh, to comfort you...

Oh, to comfort you
like your worn blue cardigan
like your favorite tea

*Sipping on cotton*

lolling in the light
blueberry summer delight
morning ease like pie
Sip on cotton clouds
while you dance on fields of blue
Summer sings for crowds of light
For the youthful side of you

*Existing*

Maybe life isn't about living anymore
But existing the best you can
From moment to moment
It's all we have now
Rest in the meadow
Let the valley rest your bones
While you are safe and sound
Burry the rest in the ground

*dreaming I'm a Hill*

i close my eyes tight
dreaming i'm a hill so high
you couldn't miss me

*Black-tailed deer*

I look out of the window and spot a black-tailed deer
His head bowed as he nuzzles the damp grass
The sky is a powdery silver
with dashes of green peaking through
The firs look untouchable
all wrapped up in the morning mist
The water is calm and eerie today
and I pray for the deer to cross safely

*The mist was folded*

When I caught sight of the sunrise this morning
I swear to god my breath was trapped
The mist was folded
and it held the light in its grasp

## DRIFT

I write to remember
To be present before
I drift away
I drift away now and again

King Tide - journal entry

At times, there's pressure to be profound
Then I reflect on the simplest beauties around
How robins flock in winter, dressed in orange and brown
How the choppy water dances wildly in the sound
Sparkly frost covering the dawning Yule ground
A flourishing deer proudly crowed
King Tide crashing over the rocky mounds
The pressure releases, my mind at ease
As I think on the brilliance of a light breeze

## ASIDE

I feel aside from everything
Unlike everyone
Maybe that's why I like it
When it's just me and the trees
They sway in a way that makes me feel free
And I'm given permission just to be

## HAPPY

Today I walked slower than I needed to
I looked up instead of at the ground
I noticed all of the little pretty sounds
The world seemed to gleam with pride
Almost like it was glad to see me
Happy that I'm here
And so I felt happy too

Decent

I don't want to be a genius
I just want to be decent

## SHEEP

I just saw a truckload of sheep
Their heads poking out like happy dogs sniffing air
I refuse to believe they won't like where they are going
I desperately need to be told they are okay
They have no idea who i am
But I smiled at them anyway

All That We Let Go

I don't know yet why I am here
but I know I am on my way to finding out
A new year is on the horizon and that terrifies
yet fuels me with hope
There has always been something so powerful
about the Great Unknown
Let's make a toast to all we hold
And all that we let go

# THREE

# *Homesick*

Am I homesick?

I'm homesick for car rides where we would sing eighties songs with the windows down

I'm homesick for family dinners with warm Summer nights and bonfires

I'm homesick for sleepovers and popcorn and face masks and rom-coms

I'm homesick for childhood

For our dogs when they were puppies

For a time before

MOTH

Will I lose a part of me

When I grow and bloom

Like a moth, do I change

Once I leave my cocoon

Winter Storms

The wind howls as it flies through the January sky
At night I feel frightened by the loud cries
But to watch as the trees stand without alarm
And rocks shield the shore from any harm
I begin to embrace the beauty and wonder of the storm
And rest in the safety and warmth of our home

## November 20

Today I miss grandma's house
The safety I felt
The instant comfort
I miss the coffee and tea
I miss weekend breakfasts
I haven't had many places in my life
where I feel truly comfortable being myself
To say whatever is on my mind
I wish I had nothing big to worry about
I wish I could just curl up on her couch

When I inhale deeply, bringing my chest forward
My sternum pops
A quiet little crack
I am reminded then, now, that I am fragile
I am bones
Skin
Cells
I am aging
Dying
Every second
But when I breathe, I am also aware
That I am living
Growing
Aching
And striving
To live longer
I'm human
A human with a popping sternum

I get nervous when I feel good
because I know how short-lived and fragile
happiness can be
I don't want to disappoint them
But more than anything
I don't want to lose myself

From time to time,
I miss home
I miss my favorite shops
My old job
I miss the people that I know
Familiar places
Friendly faces
Comfort in the known

I needed this. To remember that my legs can take me to where I want to go. I can see new things alone. I can treat myself to a coffee and just enjoy it with a stunning view. I can do things for myself. I don't have to stay home and feel stuck and sad and depressed and anxious and all the negative feelings. Just doing this small thing has made me feel a million times better. The sunshine, the fresh air, and the sounds of other people's voices. To see new things. I'm happy and I made myself happy.

I'm learning to love being alone
lost
not searching
only observing
I'm learning to feel at home
at peace
at ease
Okay with being away

It's so easy to miss my routine
Even parts of quarantine

I long for the smell of sweet summer grass

laying under my favorite tree

there were three

one for each of us to climb

When I'm barefoot on hot concrete i miss you

i miss spinning around watching the clouds become cotton candy

i drink a coke and cry because it tastes like innocence and imagination

bored nights and pointless fights

i miss sprinklers and slip 'n slides

so i stand on my sidewalk and stare at the sky

smelling the grass and cry

## To Be Here

Sometimes I look around and wonder if I made a mistake
I am so far away
But I look at the birds that surround me
The water
The trees
And I know I am so lucky to see these things
To be here in this place

# FOUR

## *Car Window Thoughts*

## STOIC RIVER

Warm candles glow and flicker
warm and soft from all corners of my sanctuary.
I sit idle at my desk.
Not a book cracked and no ink has been bled.
I come here to feel studious or stoic,
but underneath my mask of stillness,
there is a raging river flooding through my veins.
I am too afraid to take that path into the untold...
*What if they don't like me?*

# SO WHAT, I DAYDREAM

So what, I daydream?
There are endless rows of sky in my brain
Buckets and barrels of colorful paint
I can be anywhere I want with just a blink
So what, I daydream?
I'm free to go and come as I please

## PAUSE

Can't we just stop for a minute
For a day
For a year
Until we can call catch our breaths

Derealization

Sometimes I feel as though i'm not real
Or maybe that I am not alive *enough*
I know now this is a condition
Another mental disorder to manage
To cope
To forage for hope
To humble me further
To never lose sight that I'm only mortal

## Mountain Range

I could never be a mountain range,
With wide arms stretched for your embrace
I could never be a cloud bank,
With a quilt to cushion your fall from grace

A man with an interesting grey hat feeds the ducks as if he and the flock are great old friends. They are thrilled to see him, and not at all shy to say hello.

The Wednesday before Thanksgiving

Crying to Maya Hawke in the coffee shop
on the Wednesday before Thanksgiving Day
Don't worry it's all inside as I disassociate
How can I enjoy my breakfast knowing
that someone's loved one just passed away
Being an empath is especially hard around the holidays

When Writing Was Breathing

Two years have passed and now I'm afraid
I don't know how to do this anymore
We're still not out of the woods yet
My views on life and reality have shifted since we last met
It was so much easier then
When writing was breathing

to walk like that:

Imposter syndrome strikes back
As soon as I straighten the curve in my back
Who am I to walk like that

car window thoughts:

I think I write to know myself
Or maybe I am desperate
to be understood
to be seen
To know what it means to be me

*Boundaries*

Don't feel guilty for saying no
to the things that no longer serve you
You can't pour from an empty cup
Not that you owe anyone your water
Especially not those who drain you of it

# EXISTING

Maybe life isn't about living anymore
But existing the best you can
From moment to moment
It's all we have now
Rest in the meadow
Let the valley rest your bones
While you are safe and sound
Burry the rest in the ground

Honey scented beeswax candle gently flickers
I find it difficult not to watch. Flames are so mesmerizing to me. I don't understand fire but I know I am grateful for its warmth.

Steam rises from my bathtub and I finally lean back to let my shoulders rest. I've held so much tension in my body recently. It's the third day of my cycle and the past two days have been exhausting and painful and I'm so happy to be relaxing. I know it's an enormous privilege to be soaking in piping-hot water on a Friday afternoon. I don't take this luxury for granted. I give thanks for this solitude, this shelter, this warmth. I am safe and happy and I have all I need.

As a new year in my life approaches I want to take the time to slow down, enjoy the little things, and remember to enjoy them graciously. Life is incredibly precious. This I know well and I've seen it proved more so lately. Wherever you are on our planet, I hope you stop to give thanks for all the little pleasures you have that aren't so small to others. Gratitude can be challenging to find sometimes but practice searching for it can really make the days feel easier to make the most of when you feel like you're maybe in a rut or stuck on an uphill climb.

I blow the flame out, but not before closing my eyes to offer a prayer for those without light.

BE

I don't think I am supposed to know who i am anymore
I am just supposed to be

New Year:
My only resolution this year is to be happy. Safe. Good.

Blue Hydrangea

We have a large hydrangea bush
outside the living room window
I've watched it change through the Seasons
June
July
August
September
October
November
and December, too
and there is still a single blue flower
It hasn't dared to fade
It's held on through it all
It stood through the frost and the Fall
How does she do it?

Coral Light, Smokey Purple

This early morning the ground is covered
in a thin layer of crunchy white frost
The sun is brightly burning with coral light
and the clouds below are smokey purple
It looks as though there may have been a fire in the night
Strange to think of
when everything is so icy cold

*Slug*

I have never felt more human
than i do when i am in the forest
Surrounded by moss and slugs

We were once treading water:

Sometimes life can seem impossible
Sometimes the world seems unforgiving
But remember when we were out at sea
Praying for a raft or float
A sign or sense of coming hope
We are on land once again, dear
And there is the sun on the horizon
Hold my hand and remember
We were once treading water
We are only growing stronger

# A HEART

There are times when I feel like I have nothing to say
Nothing that hasn't already been said
Nothing that is worth saying
But I remember that I am the only person
who has a mind just like me
A heart that beats the same
Surely that counts for something

444

I think the universe is speaking to me through numbers
Time stamps
Mailboxes
Seconds on the microwave
Why else would certain numbers
look like home?
When I see them I know
Someone is trying to reach me

It may not feel like it now, but someone thinks you look like Autumn when the leaves turn golden and the moon grows full, lighting up the night. There is comfort found even in the Fall, and beauty that lies beneath it all.

Rowan J. Paige, author of the novella *Strawberry Milk* and poetry collection *Whilst Gazing Through a Window*, is an indie poet from the Alabama countryside, currently living in the Pacific North West amongst pine trees and crashing Atlantic waves.

She enjoys hiking, bird watching, reading, and drinking lots of coffee. Rowan often writes about love, nature, neuro-divergence, and mental health.

Instagram: @rowanpaige.writes
Email: RowanPaige.Contact@gmail.com